Six Sigma LSSGB

CW01563705

Lean Six Sigma Green Belt Exam

Version: 5.0

QUESTION NO: 1

Which element of waste best describes "the unnecessary movement of materials and/or goods"?

A.
Overprocessing

B.
Motion

C.
Conveyance

D.
Correction

Answer: C

QUESTION NO: 2

Which element of waste best describes "the cost of an idle resource"?

A.
Waiting

B.
Motion

C.
Inventory

D.
Correction

Answer: A

QUESTION NO: 3

The proper functioning of a Visual Factory is dependent upon which of these?

A.
Technically skilled workers

B.
Work space with active 5S

C.
Availability of visual tools

D.
Breakthrough projects

Answer: C

QUESTION NO: 4

Lean focuses on the sequence of activities and work required to produce a product or a service. This flow is called a_____.

A.
Value-add Flow

B.
Production Map

C.
Value Stream

D.
Operating Procedure

Answer: C

QUESTION NO: 5

Lean Enterprise is based on the premise that anywhere work is being done which of these is also occurring?

A.
Money is being spent

B.
Waste is being generated

C.
People are producing value added product

D.
Waste is being eliminated

Answer: B

QUESTION NO: 6

When constructing a Fishbone Diagram using the_____approach is the most classic arrangement.

A.
6M

B.
4M

C.
5M

D.
Alphabetical

Answer: A

QUESTION NO: 7

The 5 Why Analysis is only useful if the possible independent variable can be broken down into five possible causes.

A.
True

B.
False

Answer: B

QUESTION NO: 8

The purpose of a Process Map is to identify the complexity of the process and to assist in identifying critical steps in the process.

A.
True

B.
False

Answer: A

QUESTION NO: 9

The very best way to begin an effort to map a process is to do which of these?

A.
Interview the process owner

B.
Interview the manager of the department

C.
Walk the actual process from beginning to end

D.
Take pictures of the factory floor at each shift

Answer: C

QUESTION NO: 10

The X-Y Diagram is a tool used to identify/collate potential X's and assess their relative impact on multiple Y's.

A.
True

B.
False

Answer: A

QUESTION NO: 11

The term FMEA is an abbreviation for Failures Measure Effective Automation.

A.
True

B.
False

Answer: B

QUESTION NO: 12

When utilizing Statistics the population is defined as a collection of all the individual data points of interest.

A.
True

B.
False

Answer: A

QUESTION NO: 13

Which of these is Discrete data?

A.
Train arrived at 4:17 pm.

B.
Race car consumed 23 gallons of fuel.

C.
Of the 42 people on the bus, 12 went into the station.

D.
It took 3 hours and 32 minutes to complete the marathon.

Answer: C

QUESTION NO: 14

Nominal Scale data consists of names, labels or categories and cannot be arranged in any mathematical ordering scheme. Complex arithmetic functions cannot be easily applied to Nominal Data:

A.
True

B.
False

Answer: A

QUESTION NO: 15

When looking at a distribution graph, the Mean is defined as the_____.

A.
Average based on the sample size

B.
Aggression measured

C.
Total sample size

D.
Measurement based off a quarter of the sample size

Answer: A

QUESTION NO: 16

The difference between the largest observation and the smallest observation in the data set is known as the_____.

A.
Breadth

B.
Range

C.
Spread

D.
Median

Answer: B

QUESTION NO: 17

The Empirical Rule is important because it provides an estimate of the probability of an event occurring depending on the Standard Deviation from the Mean.

A.
True

B.

False

Answer: A

QUESTION NO: 18

The Z score is a measure of the distance in Standard Deviations of a sample data point from the Median of the sample population.

A.
True

B.
False

Answer: B

QUESTION NO: 19

Long-term Data represents all the variation that one can expect within the subject process.

A.
True

B.
False

Answer: A

QUESTION NO: 20

If a Histogram displays two peaks the distribution would likely be_____.

A.
Transformed

B.
Multi-skewed

C.
Bimodal

D.
Bi-attribute

Answer: C

QUESTION NO: 21

A Belt gathered the following defect data for a shoe production line and wanted to assemble it into a Pareto Chart. The correct order from left to right in the chart would be:

Data:

Cutting38

Forming17

Stitching56

Sealing42

A.
Forming, Sealing, Cutting, Stitching

B.
Sealing, Stitching, Forming, Cutting

C.
Stitching, Sealing, Cutting, Forming

D.
Forming, Cutting, Sealing, Stitching

Answer: C

QUESTION NO: 22

Measurement error is defined as the effect of all sources of measurement variability that caused an observed or measured value to deviate from the_____.

A.
Standard Deviation

B.
Mean

C.
Median

D.
True value

Answer: D

QUESTION NO: 23

Measurement System Analysis is a procedure used to quantify variation of the method or system used for taking measurements.

A.
True

B.
False

Answer: A

QUESTION NO: 24

The Accuracy of a Measurement System addresses_____.

A.
Stability, Bias & Linearity

B.
Repeatability & Reproducibility

C.
Stability & Sensitivity

D.
Precision & Sensitivity

Answer: A

QUESTION NO: 25

As a type of measurement error, Linearity describes a change in accuracy through the expected operating range of the measurement instrument.

A.
True

B.
False

Answer: A

QUESTION NO: 26

The deviation of the measured value from the actual value is known as_____.

A.
Bias

B.
Linearity

C.
Repeatability

D.
Movement

Answer: A

QUESTION NO: 27

The ability to repeat the same measurement obtained with one measurement instrument used several times by one appraiser while measuring the identical characteristic on the same part is known as_____.

A.
Repeatability

B.
Bias

C.
Linearity

D.
Reproducibility

Answer: A

QUESTION NO: 28

Process Capability is a function of which of these?

A.
Customer requirements

B.
Process performance

C.
Output over time

D.

All of these answers are correct

Answer: D

QUESTION NO: 29

Which of these are correct if Cpk Upper is 2.0 and Cpk Lower is 1.0?

A.
The process is not stable.

B.
The process is shifted to the left.

C.
Cpk must be reported as 1.0.

D.
The process Mean is 1.5.

Answer: C

QUESTION NO: 30

A Stable process is a process whose output is consistent over time. A primary tool used to analyze Stability would be a_____.

A.
Data Forward Plot

B.
Bag Plot

C.
Min/Max Plot

D.
Time Series Plot

Answer: D

QUESTION NO: 31

Conducting a viable Capability Analysis using Attribute Data one must obtain a fairly large sample set to be statistically sound.

A.
True

B.
False

Answer: A

QUESTION NO: 32

This output is what type of advanced Capability Analysis?

A.
Continuous

B.
Binomial

C.
Poisson

D.
Discreet

E.
DPU

Answer: B

QUESTION NO: 33

An Xbar-R chart shows a decreasing range. What can you conclude?

A.
The Mean is decreasing

B.
The Standard Deviation is increasing

C.
The Variability is decreasing

D.
The Mean is increasing

Answer: C

QUESTION NO: 34

Some of the approaches used in Lean include station warning lights, tool boards and jidohka devices in order that which of these apply?

A.
Workers do not utilize individual methods of cleaning

B.
Problems are made highly visible

C.
Work stoppages are documented properly

D.
Lessen the amount of employee pilferage

Answer: B

QUESTION NO: 35

Examples of a Visual Factory include which of these? (Note: There are 2 correct answers).

A.
White outlines on floor for proper inventory placement

B.
Documented procedures with a numerical outline

C.
Bad/Good indications of gauge readings with red and green outlines

D.
Implementing a defect inspection device

Answer: A&C

QUESTION NO: 36

Standardized work instructions apply to which resource in the process of interest?

A.
People

B.
Machines

C.
Supervision

D.
Engineering

Answer: A

QUESTION NO: 37

The Purchase Orders for Glenn Manufacturing Company were being copied by an employee and sent to four different departments yet only one department took an action based on the information in the PO. This is an example of_____.

A.
External Failure Costs

B.
Appraisal Costs

C.
Internal Failure Costs

D.
Prevention Costs

Answer: C

QUESTION NO: 38

As part of a Visual Factory plan Kanban cards are created and utilized to identify areas in need of cleaning and organization.

A.
True

B.
False

Answer: B

QUESTION NO: 39

Kanbans work best with pull systems for determining the timing of which products or services are produced.

A.
True

B.
False

Answer: A

QUESTION NO: 40

The practice of utilizing Poka-Yoke is also known as_____.

A.
Thorough integration

B.
Mistake proofing

C.
Onsite inspection

D.
Lean controls

Answer: B

QUESTION NO: 41

Examples of Mistake Proofing for a laptop computer include which of these? (Note: There are 2 correct answers).

A.
USB connection for a mouse

B.
Open/Close button for CD Drive

C.

Battery alignment pins

D.
On/Off switch for computer

Answer: A&C

QUESTION NO: 42

The Purchase Orders for Glenn Manufacturing Company were being copied by an employee and sent to four different departments yet only one department took an action based on the information in the PO. This is an example of_____.

A.
External Failure Costs

B.
Appraisal Costs

C.
Internal Failure Costs

D.
Prevention Costs

Answer: C

QUESTION NO: 43

The reason(s) for not marking the customer Specification Limits (SL) on a Control Chart is which of these? (Note: There are 4 correct answers).

A.
Process control teams should not control a process based on SLs

B.
Displaying the SLs on a Control Chart sends a wrong signal toward process control

C.

Marking the SLs on a Control Chart is against the principle of charting

D.
By marking the SLs, one can confuse the operator as to what limits are critical

E.
By using mere Control Limits the process only needs to be in Statistical Control

Answer: A, B, D&E

QUESTION NO: 44

Cost of Poor Quality (COPQ) can be classified as either Tangible (Visible) Costs or Hidden Costs.

A.
True

B.
False

Answer: A

QUESTION NO: 45

SPC charts typically have the most recent data point on the right hand side.

A.
True

B.
False

Answer: A

QUESTION NO: 46

Which of these statements describe an undesirable situation when implementing SPC? (Note: There are 2 correct answers).

A.
The lower Control Limit for the R chart is equal to zero

B.
The Control Limits are wider than the customer specification limits

C.
A process is in Statistical Control before implementation of SPC

D.
Attempt to use SPC for tracking transaction times at a warehouse

E.
Indication of the specification limits on the Control Chart

Answer: B&E

QUESTION NO: 47

If a process has Outliers which pair of charts is most preferable if subgroups will exist for the Continuous Data?

A.
Individual-Moving Range

B.
Xbar-R Charts

C.
Xbar-S Charts

D.
nP and P Charts

Answer: B

QUESTION NO: 48

Customers make a purchase decision based on a number of factors. In Lean Six Sigma we refer to these decision points as CTQ's which stands for_____.

A.
Cost of the quantity

B.
Conscious thought qualities

C.
Conspicuous time quandaries

D.
Critical-to-quality

Answer: D

QUESTION NO: 49

A process can be defined as a repetitive and systematic series of steps or activities where inputs are modified or assembled to achieve a_____result.

A.
Revenue total

B.
Month end

C.
Customer desired

D.
Budgeted

Answer: C

QUESTION NO: 50

Six Sigma refers to a process whose output has at least 80% of its data points within +/- 6 Standard Deviations from the Mean.

A.
True

B.
False

Answer: B

QUESTION NO: 51

In the late 1980's William Smith coined the name Six Sigma for a methodology that had its origins at_____for quality related work being done there.

A.
Honeywell

B.
Allied Signal

C.
General Electric

D.
Motorola

Answer: D

QUESTION NO: 52

Training cost $6,500 and a project required an initial investment of $47,500. If the project yields monthly savings of $3,500 beginning after 4 months, what is the payback period in months, before money costs and taxes?

A.
9.7

B.
15.4

C.
19.4

D.
23.7

Answer: C

QUESTION NO: 53

The acronym for the defined approach taken by Lean Six Sigma to solve significant challenges related to a process is which of these?

A.
DOE

B.
DMAIC

C.
SIPOC

D.
FMEA

Answer: B

QUESTION NO: 54

Voice of the Customer is a Lean Six Sigma technique to determine _____ attributes of a product or service.

A.
At least 6

B.
The profitable

C.
Critical-to-Quality

D.
The majority of the

Answer: C

QUESTION NO: 55

Typically a person who is trained to the skill level of a Black Belt is nearly 80% dedicated to applying Lean Six Sigma methodologies towards process solutions.

A.
True

B.
False

Answer: B

QUESTION NO: 56

Which of these is Discrete data?

A.
The airplane needed 34 gallons of fuel.

B.
The bus arrived at 12:31 pm.

C.
6 of 32 pupils failed the exam.

D.
His marathon time was 3:12.

Answer: C

QUESTION NO: 57

A Belt gathered the following defect data for a shoe production line and wanted to assemble it into a Pareto Chart. The correct order from left to right in the chart would be:

Data:Frame 32

Handle 41

String 17

Grip 23

A.
String, Grip, Frame, Handle

B.
Frame, String, Grip, Handle

C.
Handle, Frame, Grip, String

D.
String, Frame, Grip, Handle

Answer: C

QUESTION NO: 58

For a Cpk value of 1.67 and Cp value of 1, what can be concluded?

A.
This process is centered but contains variation

B.
Process is well centered and variation is also low

C.
Process is not centered and has wide variation

D.
There is a calculation error

Answer: B

QUESTION NO: 59

A plastic box manufacturer is producing 4 types of boxes. A quality engineer is working on reducing the variances of the storage capacity of boxes. To explain the variation of storage capacity across all types of boxes, which method should he use?

A.
Random sampling

B.
Stratified random sampling

C.
Systematic sampling

D.
All of these answers are correct

Answer: D

QUESTION NO: 60

In determining a 'process average fraction defective' using inductive or inferential statistics, we are making inferences about_____based on_____taken from_____.

A.
Statistics, samples, populations

B.
Population, samples, statistics

C.
Population, samples, populations

D.
Sample, statistics, population

Answer: B

QUESTION NO: 61

In a Hypothesis Test for Means, a sample size of 20 has produced a Mean of 9.5 mm with a Standard Deviation of 0.5 mm. The customer specification on the part is 10 mm. At 5%

significance level, what should the customer do?

A.
Reject the lot

B.
Accept the lot

C.
State the population Mean is greater than 10 mm

D.
Change their specification to 9.5 mm

Answer: B

QUESTION NO: 62

A Linear Regression model shows an R^2 (adjusted) of 0.90 and a P-value of 0.002. A Quadratic Regression model of the same data shows an R^2 (adjusted) of 0.92 and a P-value of 0.000. What can you conclude?

A.
A linear model would be better than a quadratic model.

B.
A quadratic model would be better than a linear model.

C.
Any non-linear model would fit the data well.

D.
Any linear or non-linear model would fit the data well.

E.
Neither a linear or non-linear model fits the data well.

F.
The Residuals would be expected to be large for either a linear or quadratic.

Answer: D

QUESTION NO: 63

With the use of Statistics we define the population to be a large enough sample set of data such that you can analyze it and draw conclusions as to all of the data.

A.
True

B.
False

Answer: B

QUESTION NO: 64

When creating a Cause and Effect Diagram the team needs to continually broaden their view as well as drill down until they identify all the potential_____impacting their process.

A.
Line operators

B.
Root Causes

C.
Inventory issues

D.
Customer requests

Answer: B

QUESTION NO: 65

Hypothesis Testing can help avoid high costs of experimental efforts by using existing data.

A.
True

B.
False

Answer: A

QUESTION NO: 66

Hypothesis Tests determine the probabilities of differences between observed data and the hypothesis being solely due to chance. This is determined based on the result of the _____.

A.
Random acts

B.
P-values

C.
Standard Deviations

D.
R-values

Answer: B

QUESTION NO: 67

It is a Type I error if we reject the Null Hypothesis when it is actually true.

A.
True

B.
False

Answer: A

QUESTION NO: 68

The purpose of a Process Map is to identify the complexity of the process and to record all actions and decision points in the process.

A.
True

B.
False

Answer: A

QUESTION NO: 69

Having an Alpha of .05 and a Beta of .10 are the most common risk levels when running a Statistical test.

A.
True

B.
False

Answer: A

QUESTION NO: 70

Use of the_____approach is the most classic arrangement when constructing a Fishbone Diagram.

A.
Chronological

B.
6M

C.
5M

D.
Alphabetical

Answer: B

QUESTION NO: 71

The deviation of the measured value from the actual value regardless of the operator is known as
_____.

A.
Linearity

B.
· Bias

C.
Repeatability

D.
Movement

Answer: B

QUESTION NO: 72

A 1-Sample t-test is used to compare an expected population Mean to a target.

A.
True

B.
False

Answer: A

QUESTION NO: 73

Unequal Variances can be the result of differing types of distributions.

A.

True

B.
False

Answer: A

QUESTION NO: 74

Due to excessive pollution, GREEN Solutions Inc. is considering subsidizing public transportation to work for its employees. According to the manager it takes an average weekday commute of 39 minutes with a Standard Deviation of 7 minutes for the employees to get to work while they use their personal vehicles for their office commute while the management set a policy of not more than 40 minutes for their daily one-way commute. A survey conducted one day on 70 employees showed an average of 34 minutes commuting time using the metro public transportation system with a Standard Deviation of 21 minutes. Assuming a Normal Distribution for the commute times by either personal or public transportation, which of these is true?

A.
The probability that they would arrive on time using personal vehicles is much higher than using the metro public transportation system (MPTS)

B.
The probability that they would arrive on time using the MPTS is much higher than using their personal vehicles

C.
The two probabilities are about the same excepting in one case the consistency is higher than the other

D.
We need to compile more data around weekends to incorporate for traffic differences

E.
When Standard Deviation is higher the probability goes down and so the MPTS is worse

Answer: B

QUESTION NO: 75

According to a manager it takes an average weekday commute of 39 minutes with a Standard Deviation of 7 minutes for the employees to get to work when they use their personal vehicles for their office commute while management set a policy of not more than 40 minutes for their daily one-way commute. A survey conducted one day on 70 employees showed an average of 34 minutes commuting time using the metro public transportation system with a Standard Deviation of 21 minutes. For the employees choosing to increase their chances to come on time using personal transportation their variation should be reduced to_____?

A.
1 minute

B.
6 minutes

C.
3.5 minutes

D.
Eliminate it to 0.0 minutes

Answer: C

QUESTION NO: 76

According to a manager it takes an average weekday commute of 39 minutes with a Standard Deviation of 7 minutes for the employees to get to work while they use their personal vehicles for their office commute while the management set a policy of not more than 40 minutes for their daily one-way commute. A survey conducted one day on 70 employees showed an average of 34 minutes commuting time using the metro public transportation system with a Standard Deviation of 21 minutes. If the Standard Deviation is uncontrollable then the other option to increase the probability of coming in on time via personal vehicles to work could be_____?

A.
Increase the average time of commute

B.
Maintain the average time of commute and change route to work

C.
Reduce average commute time to work by departing earlier

D.
Change policy at work and request for flexible times based on location

Answer: C

QUESTION NO: 77

Which element of waste best describes the cost of a resource being in the queue?

A.
Waiting

B.
Motion

C.
Inventory

D.
Correction

Answer: A

QUESTION NO: 78

The reported Cpk for a process with an average of 94 units, a spread of 22 units and upper and lower specification limits of 125 and 80 units would be?

A.
0.64

B.
1.27

C.
1.84

D.
2.12

Answer: B

QUESTION NO: 79

In order to standardize project savings financial calculation such project benefits can be compared the financial savings are typically calculated over what period of time?

A.
12 months

B.
24 months

C.
The remainder of the calendar year

D.
The remainder of the fiscal year

Answer: A

QUESTION NO: 80

Contingency Tables are used to do which of these? (Note: There are 2 correct answers).

A.
Illustrate one-tail proportions.

B.
Compare more than two sample proportions with each other.

C.
Contrast the Outliers under the tail.

D.
Analyze the "what if" scenario.

E.
Applicable to data that is Attribute in nature

Answer: B&E

QUESTION NO: 81

The following Business Case is constructed properly.

"During fiscal year 2008 the warranty returns for electric razor Model 312 were 1.3%. This represents a gap of 0.5% over target costing the company $18,500 per month."

A.
True

B.
False

Answer: A

QUESTION NO: 82

The higher the sigma level of a process the better the performance.

A.
True

B.
False

Answer: A

QUESTION NO: 83

The Six Sigma methodology had its origins at_____in the late 1980's when William Smith coined the name for quality related work being done there.

A.
Motorola

B.
Allied Signal

C.
General Electric

D.
Honeywell

Answer: A

QUESTION NO: 84

Training cost is $4,000 and a project required an initial investment of $30,000. If the project yields monthly savings of $2,000 beginning after 3 months, what is the payback period in months (before money costs and taxes)?

A.
10

B.
20

C.
27

D.
33

Answer: B

QUESTION NO: 85

Lean Six Sigma's general approach to solving significant challenges related to a process is called

_____.

A.
DOE

B.
SIPOC

C.
DMAIC

D.
FMEA

Answer: C

QUESTION NO: 86

Voice of the Customer is a Lean Six Sigma technique to determine _____ attributes of a product or service.

A.
At least 6

B.
The profitable

C.
Critical-to-Quality

D.
The majority of the

Answer: C

QUESTION NO: 87

Those who are trained to the skill levels of a Black Belt are typically utilized to apply Lean Six Sigma methodologies what percentage of their time?

A.
25%

B.
50%

C.
75%

D.
100%

Answer: D

QUESTION NO: 88

A process can be defined as a repetitive and systematic series of steps or activities where inputs are modified or assembled to achieve a customer desired result.

A.
True

B.
False

Answer: A

QUESTION NO: 89

Customers make a purchase decision based on a number of factors. In Lean Six Sigma we refer to these decision points as CTQ's or as_____.

A.
Critical-to-quality

B.
Conscious thought qualities

C.
Conspicuous time quandaries

D.
Cost of the quantity

Answer: A

QUESTION NO: 90

Cost of Poor Quality (COPQ) can be classified as Tangible (Visible) Costs and Hidden Costs.

A.
True

B.
False

Answer: A

QUESTION NO: 91

An employee of ACME Corporation noticed that every loan application that gets approved is copied four times and is stored in different locations in the company for no apparent reason. This would be an example of_____.

A.
Internal Failure Costs

B.
Appraisal Costs

C.
External Failure Costs

D.
Prevention Costs

Answer: A

QUESTION NO: 92

The 80:20 rule is associated with which of these tools?

A.
Pareto Chart

B.
Simon's Cross-Functional Tool

C.
SIPOC

D.
Framing Tool

Answer: A

QUESTION NO: 93

One of the metrics commonly used in Lean Six Sigma is DPU. This acronym stands for
_____.

A.
Deferred planned usage

B.
Defects per unit

C.
Decreased production utilization

D.
Downtime per unit

Answer: B

QUESTION NO: 94

According to the definition of Rolled Throughput Yield which of these items best describe the purpose of RTY?

A.
A function of Y=f(x)

B.
Accounts for losses due to rework and scrap

C.
Isolates the increase throughput

D.
Determines incremental Growth

Answer: B

QUESTION NO: 95

What is the Cycle Time, in seconds, for a process having a Throughput of 7,200 units per hour?

A.
0.5

B.
2

C.
4

D.
10

Answer: A

QUESTION NO: 96

The following Business Case is constructed properly.

"In business unit A there are too many flashlight returns and flashlight sales have decreased by 25 percent."

A.
True

B.
False

Answer: B

QUESTION NO: 97

To create standardization of financial benefit calculations project savings are typically based on savings over what period of time?

A.
6 months

B.
12 months

C.
24 months

D.
The remainder of the calendar year

E.
The remainder of the fiscal year

Answer: B

QUESTION NO: 98

The essence of Lean is to concentrate effort on removing waste while improving process flow to achieve speed and agility at lower cost.

A.
True

B.
False

Answer: A

QUESTION NO: 99

Lean had its origins in the development and practice of the_____Production System.

A.
Honda

B.

Toyota

C.
Ford

D.
Motorola

Answer: B

QUESTION NO: 100

Lean removes many forms of_____so Six Sigma can focus on reducing
_____.

A.
Waste, variability

B.
Inventory, defects

C.
Waste, cost

D.
Movement, variation

Answer: A

QUESTION NO: 101

The use of station warning lights, tool boards and jidohka devices in the application of Lean
accomplish which of these principles?

A.
Pilferage Minimization

B.
Visual Factory

C.
Management Awareness

D.

Operator Attentiveness

Answer: B

QUESTION NO: 102

A Lean Principle that addresses efficiency by the process worker is called
_____?

A.
Visual Factory

B.
Supervising

C.
Training

D.
Standardizing

Answer: D

QUESTION NO: 103

While management of a company must set the stage for all improvement efforts, which of these 5S's is primarily driven by management?

A.
Straighten

B.
Sort

C.
Shine

D.
Sustain

Answer: D

QUESTION NO: 104

As part of a Visual Factory plan_____cards are created and utilized to identify areas in need of cleaning and organization.

A.
Kanban

B.
Kaizen

C.
Poke-Yoke

D.
WhoSai

Answer: A

QUESTION NO: 105

The use of Kanbans work best with pull systems for determining the timing of which products or services are produced.

A.
True

B.
False

Answer: A

QUESTION NO: 106

When a Belt applies the practice of Poka-Yoke to a project challenge she is attempting to make certain the activity is_____.

A.
Well documented

B.
Removed from the line

C.
Mistake proofed

D.
Highly visible

Answer: C

QUESTION NO: 107

The Lean Principle action in the 5S approach that deals with having those items needed regularly at hand and those items need less regularly stored out of the way is known as_____.

A.
Shining

B.
Standardizing

C.
Sustaining

D.
Sorting

Answer: D

QUESTION NO: 108

SPC on the outputs is more preferred than SPC on the inputs when implementing SPC for your process.

A.
True

B.
False

Answer: B

QUESTION NO: 109

Significant variation in process performance is a consequence of several causes that can be classified using which of the terminologies shown. (Note: There are 2 correct answers).

A.
Common

B.
Random

C.
Uneducated

D.
Special

E.
Vital

Answer: A&D

QUESTION NO: 110

When it comes to Control one of the most effective means of eliminating defects is to

_____.

A.
Train personnel often and thoroughly

B.
Keep a Six Sigma project going on the process at all times

C.
Design defect prevention into the product

D.
Have each process consist of no more than five steps

Answer: C

QUESTION NO: 111

A periodic time frame can be used to arrange for Control Limit and Center Line calculations with good SPC implementation in a process.

A.
True

B.
False

Answer: A

QUESTION NO: 112

The data on SPC charts are typically constructed such that they have the most recent data point on the right hand side.

A.
True

B.
False

Answer: A

QUESTION NO: 113

Which statement(s) describe an undesirable situation when implementing SPC?

A.
The lower Control Limit for the R chart is equal to zero

B.
Attempt to use SPC for tracking transaction times at a warehouse

C.
A process is in Statistical Control before implementation of SPC

D.
The Control Limits are wider than the customer specification limits

Answer: D

QUESTION NO: 114

If a process has Outliers which pair of charts is most preferable if subgroups will exist for the Continuous Data?

A.
Individual—Moving Range

B.
Xbar-R Charts

C.
Xbar-S Charts

D.
nP and P Charts

Answer: B

QUESTION NO: 115

After a Belt has put data through the smoothing process which chart would be used to look for trends in the data?

A.
Moving Average Chart

B.
Multi-Vari Chart

C.
X bar Chart

D.
Pareto Chart

Answer: A

QUESTION NO: 116

A Belt concludes a Lean Six Sigma project with the creation of a Control Plan. At what point can the Control Plan be closed?

A.
Never, a Control Plan is a living document

B.
As soon as the Champion signs off

C.
Within 30 days of the LSS project review team meeting

D.
After the project has been presented at the recognition event

Answer: A

QUESTION NO: 117

When analyzing a data set we frequently graph one metric as a function of another. If the slope of the Correlation line is -2.5 we would say the two metrics are_____correlated?

A.
Positively

B.
Not

C.
Negatively

D.

None

Answer: C

QUESTION NO: 118

Multiple Linear Regressions (MLR) is best used when which of these are applicable? (Note: There are 3 correct answers).

A.
Non-linear relationships between the inputs X's and output Y

B.
Uncertainty in the slope of the linear relationship between an X and a Y

C.
Relationships between Y (output) and more than one X (Input)

D.
Preventing the use of a Designed Experiment if unnecessary

E.
We assume that the X's are independent of each other

Answer: C, D&E

QUESTION NO: 119

Fractional Factorial designs for an experimental approach are used when_____about the multiple metric interaction in a process.

A.
Much is known

B.
Little is known

C.
We don't care

D.
Data exists

Answer: B

QUESTION NO: 120

A Belt will occasionally do a quick experiment referred to as an OFAT which stands for
_____.

A.
Only a Few Are Tested

B.
Opposite Factors Affect Technique

C.
One Factor At a Time

D.
Ordinary Fractional Approach Technique

Answer: C

QUESTION NO: 121

Which statement(s) are correct for the Regression Analysis shown here? (Note: There are 2 correct answers).

```
Regression Analysis: HeatFlux versus %Cu, Thickness

The Regression Equation is
HeatFlux = 484 + 4.80 %Cu - 24.2 Thickness


Predictor Coef     SE Coef T      P
Constant  483.67   39.57   12.22  0.000
%Cu         4.7963  0.9511  5.04   0.000
Thickness -24.215 1.941   -12.48 0.000


S = 8.93207 R-Sq = 85.9%     R-Sq (adj) = 84.8%
Analysis of Variance
Source          DF    SS        MS      F      P
Regression       2   12607.6   6303.8  79.01  0.000
Residual Error  26   2074.3    79.8
Total           28   14681.9


Source          DF    Seq SS
%Cu              1    184.5
Thickness        1    12423.1

Unusual Observations
Obs  %Cu   HeatFlux   Fit      SE Fit  Residual  St Resid
1    40.6  271.80     274.74   5.08    -2.94     -0.40 X
22   36.3  254.50     230.91   2.39    23.59      2.74R


R denotes an observation with a large standardized residual.
X denotes an observation whose X value gives it large influence.
```

This Regression is an example of a Multiple Linear Regression.

B.
This Regression is an example of Cubic Regression.

C.
%Cu explains the majority of the process variance in heat flux.

D.
Thickness explains over 80% of the process variance in heat flux.

E.
The number of Residuals in this Regression Analysis is 26.

Answer: A,D

QUESTION NO: 122

The Regression Model for an observed value of Y contains the term which represents the Y axis intercept when X = 0.

A.
True

B.
False

Answer: A

QUESTION NO: 123

Which statement(s) are true about the Fitted Line Plot shown here? (Note: There are 2 correct answers).

A.
When Reactant increases, the Energy Consumed increases.

B.
The slope of the equation is a positive 130.5.

C.
The predicted output Y is close to -18 when the Reactant level is set to 6.

D.
Over 85 % of the variation of the Energy Consumed is explained by the Reactant via this Linear Regression.

Answer: C&D

QUESTION NO: 124

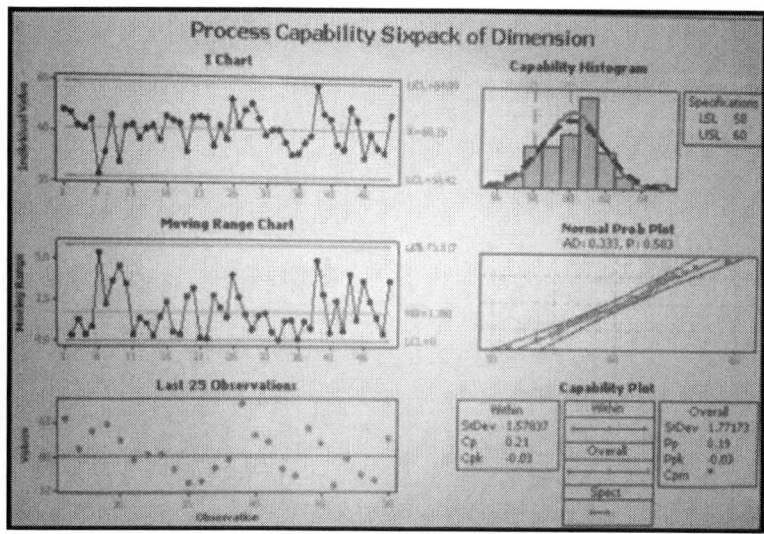

Process Capability Sixpack of Dimension

After reviewing the Capability Analysis shown here select the statement(s) that are untrue.

A.
The process is properly assumed to be a Normal process

B.
The Mean of the process moving range is 1.78

C.
The process is out of Control

D.
This Capability Analysis used subgroups

Answer: A

QUESTION NO: 125

The actual experimental response data varied somewhat from what a Belt had predicted them to be. This is the result of which of these?

A.
Inefficiency of estimates

B.

Residuals

C.
Confounded data

D.
Gap Analysis

Answer: B

QUESTION NO: 126

What is the Cycle Time, in minutes, for a process having a Throughput of 360 units per hour?

A.
0.167

B.
0.333

C.
0.667

D.
1.333

Answer: A

QUESTION NO: 127

The generation of a Regression Equation is justified when we_____. (Note: There are 4 correct answers).

A.
Expect the relationship to be Linear between the output and inputs

B.
Know that there is a non-linear relationship between output and input(s)

C.
Need to understand how to control a process output by controlling the input(s)

D.
Experience several process defects and have no other way to fix hem

E.
When it is very expensive or too late to measure the output

Answer: A, C, D&E

QUESTION NO: 128

According to the definition of Rolled Throughput Yield which of the following items best describe the purpose of RTY?

A.
A function of $Y=f(x)$

B.
Determines incremental Growth

C.
Isolates the increase throughput

D.
Accounts for rejects and reworks

Answer: D

QUESTION NO: 129

The following Business Case is constructed properly.

"During fiscal year 2008 the warranty returns for electric razor Model 312 were 1.3%. This represents a gap of 0.5% over target costing the company $18,500 per month."

A.
True

B.
False

Answer: A

QUESTION NO: 130

Which statement(s) are true about the Fitted Line Plot shown here? (Choose 2 correct answers).

A.
When Reactant increases, the Energy Consumed increases.

B.
The slope of the equation is a positive 130.5.

C.
The predicted output Y is close to -18 when the Reactant level is set to 6.

D.
Over 85 % of the variation of the Energy Consumed is explained by the Reactant via this Linear Regression.

Answer: C&D

QUESTION NO: 131

Select all the statements that are true after reviewing the Capability Analysis shown here. (Pick 4 correct answers).

A.
The process is out of Control.

B.
The process is properly assumed to be a Normal process.

C.
The Mean of the process moving range is 1.78.

D.
This Capability Analysis used subgroups.

E.
Majority of the dimensional values are outside of the tolerance than within.

Answer: B, C, D&E

QUESTION NO: 32

A Six Sigma tool that helps to screen factors by using graphical techniques to logically subgroup multiple discrete X's plotted against a continuous Y is known as a_____Chart.

A.
SIPOC

B.
Multi-Vari

C.
Box Plot

D.
Whisker

Answer: B

QUESTION NO: 133

A primary benefit of using a Multi-Vari Chart is it provides a visual presentation of two-way interactions.

A.
True

B.
False

Answer: A

QUESTION NO: 134

_____Distributions occur when data comes from several sources that are supposed to be the same yet are not.

A.
Skewed

B.
Bimodal

C.
Gaussian

D.
Tri-peaked

Answer: A

QUESTION NO: 135

Bias in Sampling is an error due to lack of independence among random samples or due to systematic sampling procedures.

A.
True

B.
False

Answer: A

QUESTION NO: 136

To draw inferences about a sample population being studied by modeling patterns of data in a way that accounts for randomness and uncertainty in the observations is known as

_____.

A.
Influential Analysis

B.
Inferential Statistics

C.
Physical Modeling

D.
Sequential Inference

Answer: B

QUESTION NO: 137

For a Normal Distribution the Mean, Median and Mode are the same data point.

A.
True

B.
False

Answer: A

QUESTION NO: 138

When two Inputs have an impact on the Output together yet seem to have no or little impact on their own this is called a/an_____.

A.
Interaction

B.
Oddity

C.
Coincidence

D.
Impossibility

Answer: A

QUESTION NO: 139

Hypothesis Testing can save time and help avoid high costs of experimental efforts by using existing data.

A.
True

B.
False

Answer: A

QUESTION NO: 140

It is a Type II error if we decide to reject the Null Hypothesis when it is actually true.

A.
True

B.
False

Answer: B

QUESTION NO: 141

A Belt experienced an Alpha of .05 and a Beta of .10 and knew these are the most common risk levels when running a Statistical test.

A.
True

B.
False

Answer: A

QUESTION NO: 142

Inferential Statistics is largely about Significance. There are both Practical and _____
Significance to consider during an analysis of data in a Lean Six Sigma project.

A.
Problematic

B.
Impractical

C.
Usable

D.
Statistical

Answer: D

QUESTION NO: 143

The Central Limit Theorem helps us understand the_____we are taking and is the basis
for using sampling to estimate population parameters.

A.
Analysis

B.
Kurtosis

C.
Risk

D.
Route

Answer: C

QUESTION NO: 144

Hypothesis Tests determine the probabilities of differences between observed data and the hypothesis being solely due to_____based on the result of the P-values.

A.
Human error

B.
Measurement error

C.
Shift differences

D.
Chance

Answer: D

QUESTION NO: 145

The Alpha level of a test (level of significance) represents the yardstick against which P-values are measured and the Null Hypothesis is rejected if the P-value is which of these?

A.
Less than the Alpha level.

B.
Greater than the Alpha level.

C.
Greater than the Beta and Alpha level.

D.
Less than one minus Alpha.

E.
Less than the power of one minus Beta.

Answer: A

QUESTION NO: 146

A 1-Sample t-test is used when you want to compare the Median of one distribution to a target value.

A.
True

B.
False

Answer: B

QUESTION NO: 147

When a Belt is analyzing sample data she should keep in mind that 95% of Normally Distributed data is within +/- 2 Standard Deviations from the Mean.

A.
True

B.
False

Answer: A

QUESTION NO: 148

The Standard Deviation for the distribution of Means is called the_____and approaches zero as the sample size reaches 30.

A.
Standard Error

B.
Mean Deviation

C.
Mean Spread

D.
Mean Error

Answer: A

QUESTION NO: 149

Due to excessive pollution, GREEN Solutions Inc. is considering subsidizing public transportation to work for its employees. According to the manager it takes an average weekday commute of 39 minutes with a Standard Deviation of 7 minutes for the employees to get to work while they use their personal vehicles for their office commute while the management set a policy of not more than 40 minutes for their daily one-way commute. A survey conducted one day on 70 employees showed an average of 34 minutes commuting time using the metro public transportation system with a Standard Deviation of 21 minutes. Assuming a Normal Distribution for the commute times by either personal or public transportation, which of these is true?

A.
The probability that they would arrive on time using personal vehicles is much higher than using the metro public transportation system (MPTS)

B.
The probability that they would arrive on time using the MPTS is much higher than using their personal vehicles

C.
The two probabilities are about the same excepting in one case the consistency is higher than the other

D.
We need to compile more data around weekends to incorporate for traffic differences

E.
When Standard Deviation is higher the probability goes down and so the MPTS is worse

Answer: B

QUESTION NO: 150

According to a manager it takes an average weekday commute of 39 minutes with a Standard Deviation of 7 minutes for the employees to get to work when they use their personal vehicles for their office commute while management set a policy of not more than 40 minutes for their daily one-way commute. A survey conducted one day on 70 employees showed an average of 34 minutes commuting time using the metro public transportation system with a Standard Deviation of 21 minutes. For the employees choosing to increase their chances to come on time using personal transportation their variation should be reduced to_____?

A.
1 minute

B.
6 minutes

C.
3.5 minutes

D.
Eliminate it to 0.0 minutes

Answer: C

QUESTION NO: 151

According to a manager it takes an average weekday commute of 39 minutes with a Standard Deviation of 7 minutes for the employees to get to work while they use their personal vehicles for their office commute while the management set a policy of not more than 40 minutes for their daily one-way commute. A survey conducted one day on 70 employees showed an average of 34 minutes commuting time using the metro public transportation system with a Standard Deviation of 21 minutes. If the Standard Deviation is uncontrollable then the other option to increase the probability of coming in on time via personal vehicles to work could be_____?

A.
Increase the average time of commute

B.
Maintain the average time of commute and change route to work

C.
Reduce average commute time to work by departing earlier

D.
Change policy at work and request for flexible times based on location

Answer: C

QUESTION NO: 152

Which of the following is used to test the significance for the analysis of a Variance Table?

A.
t Test

B.
F Test

C.
Chi Square Test

D.
Acid Test

Answer: B

QUESTION NO: 153

Non-parametric testing is done when which of these are applicable? (Choose 3 correct answers).

A.
When the traditional t tests don't produce the results we need

B.
A Hypothesis Test for the Median of the population is in question

C.
It does not require data to come from Normally Distributed populations

D.
They look at the Median rather than the Mean of populations

E.
When there are no parameters to measure in the process

Answer: B, C&D

QUESTION NO: 154

The Mann-Whitney Test is used to test if the Means for two samples are different.

A.
True

B.
False

Answer: B

QUESTION NO: 155

Contingency Tables are used to perform which of these functions?

A.
Illustrate one-tail proportions

B.
Analyze the "what if" scenario

C.
Contrast the Outliers under the tail

D.
Compare more than two sample proportions with each other

Answer: D

QUESTION NO: 156

For the data shown here a Belt suspects the three grades are supplying the same results. Which statement(s) are true for proper Hypothesis Testing?

Grade A	Grade B	Grade C
0.917	1.1	0.63
0.68	0.173	4.17
1.74	0.24	0.6
0.3	0.67	0.84
0.33	6.94	0.22
4.13		

A.
The most appropriate Central Tendency to test is the Means

B.
An appropriate test to test Central Tendency is the Levene's test

C.
An appropriate test to test Central Tendency is the ANOVA test

D.
An appropriate test to test Central Tendency is the Mood's Median test

Answer: D

QUESTION NO: 157

If the data displayed in a Histogram displays two peaks the distribution would likely be

_____.

A.
Transformed

B.
Multi-skewed

C.
Bi-attribute

D.
Bimodal

Answer: D

QUESTION NO: 158

The_____is important because it provides an estimate of the probability of an event occurring depending on the Standard Deviation from the Mean.

A.
Shewhart Principle

B.
Pareto Rule

C.
Mean/Mode Spread

D.
Empirical Rule

Answer: D

QUESTION NO: 159

Skewed, or Mixed, Distributions occur when data comes from several sources that are supposed to be the same yet are not.

A.
True

B.
False

Answer: A

QUESTION NO: 160

Measurement System Analysis is a procedure used to quantify all_____in the method orsystem used for taking measurements.

A.
Totals

B.
People involved

C.
Variation

D.
Summations

Answer: C

QUESTION NO: 161

The FMEA is used to analyze potential source of defects in the process of interest and stands for

_____.

A.
Failure Measure for Effective Automation

B.
Failure Modes and Effect Analysis

C.
Focused Mental Efforts Analyze

D.
Failed Manufacturing Efforts Analyzed

Answer: B

QUESTION NO: 162

The perfect sample size is the minimum number of data points required to provide exactly 6% overlap or risk if one wants a 95% confidence level.

A.
True

B.
False

Answer: B

Printed in Great Britain
by Amazon

18365587R00045